Reclaim & Recover

Heal from Toxic Relationships with a 7-Step Guided Journal

Tara Blair Ball

Certified Relationship Coach

PAGE STREET
PUBLISHING CO.

dedication

For you, whoever you are, wherever you are. You're not alone.

table of contents

introduction

I woke up in my daughter's bed in my children's bedroom. The room was dark, but it'd been early afternoon when I'd crawled into it sobbing. My face felt puffy and my mouth dry. My children were with their father at the house we all used to share together, and I was alone in this tiny house I'd rented 20 minutes away.

I missed my children so desperately. I missed the life I'd had with their father, though I couldn't say I missed *him* as a person. I missed the dreams I'd had for our relationship: of raising children with the person I'd had them with, of retiring to a mountain cabin with a burbling creek outside.

I had dragged myself out of the most toxic relationship I'd ever been in, but I didn't understand why I seemed to be so much more emotional, upset, and . . . *crazier* now than I'd been while in that relationship.

Why do I feel so miserable? I asked myself again and again. *I chose to leave!*

That thought wracked me. I'd been in that relationship for nearly a decade. I'd regularly felt anxious, depressed, embarrassed, and ashamed, and I'd never felt so small and inconsequential. That relationship had clearly been like drinking poison for my spirit. But why hadn't leaving it been the cure?

Because, as I would learn later, there'd been damage I was responsible for recovering from, and I needed to replace some of the toxic habits I had learned with healthier ones.

Today, I'm a relationship coach who has helped hundreds of people recover from toxic relationships. I've guided individuals through the exact same process I'm about to guide you through in this book.

Let's dive into what I mean by a "toxic" relationship.

What Is a Toxic Relationship?

In her book *Toxic People*, Dr. Lillian Glass defines a toxic relationship as a "relationship [in which people] don't support each other, where there's conflict and one seeks to undermine the other, where there's competition, where there's disrespect and a lack of cohesiveness."

Every relationship has its peaks and valleys, but a toxic relationship will be composed of primarily negative moments. You'll regularly feel drained in the relationship, and you may even experience emotional, verbal, mental, sexual, or physical abuse. These kinds of relationships can be damaging to any of the participants, and the effects can be felt for a long time.

It's also important to note that while I will, at times, use "toxic partner" to describe your ex, I am using this only as an identifier, not as a judgment on anyone. Some people may be bad *for* you, but that doesn't mean they are inherently *bad*. They might be a perfectly wonderful person, but the mix of their issues and your issues could be like toxic sludge.

The Warning Signs of a Toxic Relationship

Most toxic relationships will involve some kind of abuse (whether verbal, emotional, mental, psychological, sexual, or physical) or persistent disrespect. But often the signs are more subtle. They also may start out subtly and escalate over time.

If you are recently out of a relationship and are unsure whether it was toxic, here are some signs to consider:

- You were constantly comparing your relationship to other couples. You may have done this either out of jealousy (*Why aren't we as happy as they are?*) or to feel like your relationship wasn't so bad (*At least my partner never does . . .*).

- You regularly felt a whole slew of negative emotions: unhappy, anxious, sad, angry. You may not understand why you felt this way, or you put the burden of changing your feelings on your partner: *If they'd just change jobs, then they'd stop complaining and we could be happy . . .*

- You changed over the course of the relationship. This may mean that you became depressed or overly anxious, isolated from friends, lost or gained weight in an unhealthy way, developed nervous traits or habits (like nail-biting), or gave up hobbies or habits you once loved (like dancing or exercising).

- You lost your sense of who you were. You used to be comfortable going anywhere alone, but after being with your partner, you became too anxious to go anywhere without them.

- Your friends and family members voiced their concerns about your relationship. Anytime someone close to us voices a concern, it should be taken seriously, but you may have not wanted to listen.

- There was any form of violence or abuse. It is important to note that abuse/violence and love cannot exist in the same relationship.

Here are some other common signs of a toxic relationship (actions true of one or both partners):

- sarcasm, criticism, and hostility as normal parts of communication
- jealousy
- controlling behaviors
- long-lasting grudges or resentments
- dishonesty
- one or both of you making decisions without considering the other
- one or both of you not voicing your needs or ignoring the needs of the other
- little to no self-care
- constantly feeling like you're walking on eggshells

If you can identify with any of the above descriptions, then this book is for you. While this book focuses on recovering from *romantic* relationships, any relationship can be toxic: ones with friends, siblings, parents, children, coworkers, etc. The tools you'll find within this book can be adapted for any toxic relationship.

Toxic relationships rob us of our serenity and security. They make us doubt our reality and make us wonder whether we are truly lovable. But we can get back our sense of self, our sense of our own possibility, by recovering.

This book is written for you if you are *out* of your toxic relationship. While toxic relationships can be fixed, it would require *both* people to put in the work. This book is not for people trying to recover their relationship, but to recover *from* their relationship. This means you have no or limited contact with your former partner. "No contact" means you do not respond to phone calls, text messages, or emails; you do not follow them on any social media platforms; and you do not speak to them at all or you're casually polite (nothing beyond small talk) when you see them in public. You also have boundaries with other people about what they share with you about your ex ("Hey, I'd really prefer not to hear anything about _____. Can we talk about something else?").

Limited contact is often necessary when you co-parent with them or have some other arrangement that must be dealt with. "Limited contact" means you would keep to specific boundaries. For example, you only discuss the children and their needs and nothing else, or only whatever you need to deal with and nothing else. If your ex brings up anything outside of those topics, then you do not respond or engage. That may seem harsh, but toxic relationships can be extremely damaging. We may not even be able to assess how much damage exists until we've had some time away from our former partner.

If you're not ready to leave and/or go no to limited contact with your toxic partner, I suggest you seek out a therapist, and if you're experiencing any kind of abuse or violence, please check out the resources available to you at thehotline.org or call them at 1-800-799-7233.

Many people also discover that once they leave a toxic relationship, they struggle with depression, anxiety, disordered eating, compulsive behaviors, suicidal thoughts or ideation, self-harm, or other mental health issues. These issues may not self-correct on their own and require professional help. Please research therapists or counselors in your area to work with you on these issues.

how to use this guided journal

I'm going to tell you something that you may not like.

I didn't like it either.

But the only way out is *through*.

Through cannot be accomplished by avoiding, denying, finding distractions, throwing yourself into work, getting a "revenge bod," jumping on dating apps, or any of the other millions of ways you can pretend that life is fine and that your healing is unnecessary.

If you need some further motivation, know that Sandra Langeslag, associate professor of behavioral neuroscience at the University of Missouri–St. Louis, said, "Distraction is a form of avoidance, which has been shown to reduce the recovery from a breakup."

Do you really want to *reduce* your recovery from your breakup? I hope not.

So to recover, you'll need to go *through*.

Through means you're going to have to address and work on some things, and it won't be all ice cream and sprinkles.

I get it. I've been there too. I didn't want to do the work of recovery because it sounded . . . hard. *Haven't I had* ENOUGH *hard?* I remember moaning to myself. *Why can't it just be EASY?*

But the parts of yourself that hurt today weren't hurt in just one moment, hour, or day. It was likely you were hurt in a million little ways over an extended period of time, by maybe not just your most recent relationship, but by other relationships before that one too.

For the sake of your future self, I hope you get the help you need and stick with this book. I hope you choose you—a better, happier, healthier you—regardless of what work you need to do to get there.

This book is divided into seven steps:

- **Step 1:** Mapping Thoughts and Feelings
- **Step 2:** Narrating Your Toxic Relationship
- **Step 3:** Developing Empathy
- **Step 4:** Softening Emotions
- **Step 5:** Accepting Personal Responsibility
- **Step 6:** Establishing Accountability
- **Step 7:** Restoring Trust

Each step was selected based on scientific research, case studies, and my own experience both as a recovering person and as a relationship coach. My goal is that each step will guide you slowly down the path toward healing.

Because each step builds on the one before it, I recommend that you work through each step in order. If you decide to rebel and skip around, I won't hold it against you. I promise I have no judgment either way, but as someone who's been there before, I hope you'll take my gentle suggestion of trying to go through this book in the way I've laid it out.

Please also consider giving yourself time to work through it. If you're like me, you may want to rush through it as quickly as possible because you just want to be done. "Done" to you may mean the same as "healed." And the sooner you get to done, the sooner you get to be healed.

But healing is a cyclical, not linear, process. The duration, frequency, and intensity of your feelings *will* lessen over time, but new things may trigger them. You may learn your former partner has moved on, and you suddenly desperately miss them or you're angry all over again. Certain special dates or holidays may upset you.

You may also find that you need a break between chapters. A certain chapter could bring up a lot of feelings, and rushing through to the next chapter may be a very unkind thing to do to yourself. Listen to your body and how you feel. Jumping into the next chapter before you're ready could result in an emotional hangover. Being gentle with yourself should be the most important thing.

Each guided prompt is followed by a set of lines, so you can write out your response. You're welcome to write as much or as little as you like. You're also welcome to write your answers on a separate sheet of paper if you feel like the space given isn't enough for all you need to write.

While I know it's hard to accept that you're here and having to work on this, I applaud you for taking this valuable step in your own healing.

All the best!

step 1:
mapping thoughts and feelings

If you're recently out of a toxic relationship or just starting to heal from it for the first time, you may relate to how I and some of my clients have described it:

- "I felt like my heart had been carved out of my chest, and I somehow had to keep on existing."
- "Like everything had been ruined and I'd never feel happiness ever again."
- "I couldn't eat or sleep. I couldn't get out of bed. It felt like every part of me, even my heart, was sick or broken."
- "I've never missed and hated someone so much at the same time."
- "One minute, I'm fine. Life is going to be great. I don't need them. The next I'm sobbing in my car because no one is ever going to love me and I'm going to die alone."
- "I took care of myself, our three children, and her plus worked a full-time job. I don't know how I used to have so much energy and now I have none."
- "I don't even know who I am anymore or even what I like."

When we leave a toxic relationship, our emotional landscape often feels as if it is in constant turmoil. We're sad. We're lonely. We're angry. We're happy. We're scared. We may feel at the mercy of our feelings because they can whip so quickly from one to the next.

We also just may feel . . . awful, and we can't pinpoint the individual emotions that are equaling our general sense of awfulness.

Without a clear idea of what we're feeling and thinking, we don't have a way to move through those feelings and choose healthy ways of managing them.

We often try to understand why we're feeling such a way, but the "why" doesn't matter as much as the "what." As in, what are you feeling? Angry? Sad? Lonely? Frustrated? Joyful?

Feelings are feelings. We often ascribe moral judgments to our feelings by naming some as "good" or "bad," but feelings just . . . are. Every feeling has both a positive and a negative to it. Yes, we may not like feeling angry, for example, but feeling angry can be a good indicator that one of our boundaries was violated and push us to be assertive in enforcing it.

When we try to understand the "why" behind something, we're often trying to control it. We think, *If I understood why I'm so angry, then I could stop being angry!* Unfortunately, we can't control how we're feeling. We can only control our actions and reactions as a result of our feelings. So while you may not be able to control your anger, you can control whether you lash out at someone or not.

Paying attention to what you're feeling and thinking is the first step in learning how to manage the effects of your feelings. Although you can't control what you feel, you can take active steps to respond to your feelings in a healthier fashion.

Let's start by looking at the range of feelings.

Dr. Gloria Willcox developed the Feeling Wheel with the primary emotions: sad, mad, scared, joyful, powerful, and peaceful. Sad, mad, and scared are considered "uncomfortable" emotions, while joyful, powerful, and peaceful are considered "comfortable" ones.

If we can identify which primary emotion we're experiencing, then we can narrow it down even further to better pinpoint what we're really feeling.

the feeling wheel

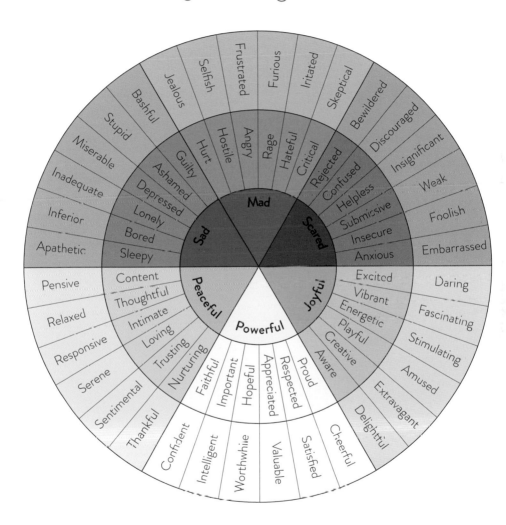

Source: https://cdn.gottman.com/wp-content/uploads/2020/12/The-Gottman-Institute_The-Feeling-Wheel_v2.pdf.

Emotional Check-In

We're going to start our work by doing an emotional check-in. Getting into this habit of self-awareness will greatly help your healing, so I encourage you to return to these questions again and again. Emotional check-ins are designed to help you pause, figure out what you're feeling, investigate what may have caused your feelings, and then consider healthy ways of handling or managing them.

Think of an emotional check-in as the first step in assessing what's truly going on. When your car starts making a weird noise, your mechanic's first job is learning all they can about the issue. When does the noise happen? What are you doing when the noise happens? What does it sound like? Where do you hear it? And so on. All of that information helps them more fully understand and isolate the issue. Then they can figure out how to fix it. Emotional check-ins work the same way!

Before beginning an emotional check-in, follow these steps:

- Close your eyes.
- Do a body scan. Pay attention to how you feel physically, from the top of your head to the bottom of your feet. Do you notice any tension? Any discomfort? Is your heart racing? Is your breathing quick and shallow?
- Take a deep breath. Breathe in through your nose and out through your mouth.

When we're getting in touch with our emotions, they often show up in our body first. We're tense when we feel stressed or anxious. Our shoulders may cave forward when we're scared or feel helpless. Having a better sense of your own body's cues can help you figure out exactly what you're feeling.

Reflection Questions

1. How are you feeling? Today or in this very moment?

2. Can you be more specific about how you're feeling? Use the Feeling Wheel (page 19) to help! Instead of just feeling "bad," do you feel overwhelmed, disappointed, or drained? It's key that you use words that clearly label how you're feeling. What physical cues in your body help you know you are feeling this way?

3. Who or what caused your feelings? There may be multiple things going on, but start with the major and work your way down. (For example, "I saw the manager for my project at work and it made me feel anxious because I am behind on it. I also didn't sleep well last night, and that's been wearing on me.")

4. Did you do anything that caused you to feel those particular feelings? (For example: "I checked their social media profile even though I knew I shouldn't" or "I didn't eat all day.")

5. If something you did caused you to feel those particular feelings, what was your motivation? Did you hope to accomplish something? Did you get what you wanted? Why or why not?

6. Did you do anything as a result of your feelings? Perhaps you talked with a friend or ate a few too many of those brownies in the break room.

Thought Check-In

Similar to an emotional check-in, a thought check-in pushes you to be more self-aware. What kind of thoughts are in your head on a regular basis?

Is your mind a "safe" place for you?

While in my toxic relationship, mine certainly wasn't. I drove home most days feeling panicky, my mind racing with thoughts like, *What kind of mood is he going to be in? What can I do to make him talk to me? If he would just get a different job, then maybe he wouldn't be so stressed and take it out on me.* I was obsessed with changing my situation, and I believed that if my toxic partner changed, then everything would be fine. All the while, I was losing myself.

After I left that relationship and prior to my recovery, my mind still wasn't a safe place. I was plagued by negative thoughts, such as *Should I have left? I'm going to ruin my children's life. Kids should have both their mom and their dad. I can't raise two kids on my own!*

It's likely you've had negative thoughts yourself, about whether you should have left or what you could have done differently to make them stay, your future, or any manner of other things. Most negative thoughts fall into certain categories.

Filtered: You ignore the positive and focus entirely on negative experiences to inform what you think.

Overgeneralizing: One bad experience becomes evidence that all of your future experiences will be the same.

Shoulds: You may have a belief on how you "should" have done something, and because you didn't do it as you "should" have, you come down hard on yourself.

All or nothing: If you see things as all good or all bad, you're preventing yourself from seeing the whole picture. Rarely do things in our lives function in absolutes. Seeing mistakes as a reason to give up ignores how you may have made real progress.

Catastrophizing: *What if the next person I date is toxic too?* If you worry that a future relationship will also be toxic, you can seek help. This book is one such way to help yourself not have a toxic relationship again in the future.

It's critical to recognize that negative thoughts are not only irrational but also unhelpful. Keeping a journal of your thoughts and emotions throughout the day can help you become more aware of what's driving you and why, as well as help to inform the rest of your healing process.

Reflection Questions

1. What negative things have you been telling yourself lately? (For example: *I'll never find another romantic partner. I can't do this.***)**

_____

_____

_____

_____

_____

_____

_____

_____

2. What caused you to think those things? Has someone told you those things before or did you hear or gather them from somewhere? Think back. Do they have a source?

step 1: mapping thoughts and feelings

3. What evidence do you have to support those thoughts? Can you really not do it alone or did you actually do it and handle yourself admirably?

_____

_____

_____

_____

_____

_____

_____

_____

_____

_____

_____

_____

_____

_____

_____

_____

_____

_____

_____

_____

_____

_____

4. What category do your thoughts generally fall into (see pages 27–28)? Why do you think that is?

_____

_____

_____

_____

_____

_____

_____

_____

_____

_____

_____

_____

_____

_____

_____

_____

_____

_____

_____

_____

_____

_____

5. Have you realized anything about your thoughts from what you've read in this section? What?

step 2:
narrating your toxic relationship

When we've had a breakup (even of a relationship that wasn't toxic), we often see our former relationship in one of two ways: all good or all bad. This might be the story we tell ourselves and others about how the relationship went. You may start most of your sentences with, "They did . . ." or "They were . . ." You may ignore your part in the relationship altogether or the parts that were actually good.

In psychology, this is called "splitting," "black-and-white thinking," or "all-or-nothing" thinking. This is considered a distortion in your thinking because it ignores that relationships, much like people, are nuanced and complex. Every relationship has its good and bad moments.

If you're recovering from a toxic relationship, it's likely that you have moments where you see your former relationship as all good or all bad. When you miss your former partner, you may remember only the good moments and fall into a puddle of grief. Or you may only remember the bad moments and throw yourself into a rage. Grief and rage are valid feelings, but you have to feel all of your feelings to truly recover.

You also need to look at your own part in your unhealthy relationship. No one person is at fault for all of the bad in a relationship. It can feel easy (and sometimes even warranted) to place all of the blame on one person, but that may not actually be true. If two people were in that relationship, likely two people had some fault. Some people's faults may be greater than others', but that doesn't make anyone completely blameless. Two wrongs don't make a right, remember?

If we place all of the blame solely on our former partner, we also won't be able to see the areas where *we* need to grow and change. All you can control at this moment is *you*. You don't want to have another toxic relationship in your future, so you can only work on what you're responsible for and can control.

This step will help you start to see your toxic relationship in a more realistic light: both the good *and* bad parts of it. It's okay if it's hard at first to answer some of these questions. Allow yourself some time to reflect, and try to be as comprehensive as possible.

A Clearer Picture of Your Toxic Relationship

The following questions will require you to reflect back on your former partner and your relationship with them. While it can be incredibly difficult to separate the past from the present, it's important that you gather up as much information as you can to get a clear picture of your time together, as well as help yourself to move toward a more whole emotional response.

Unlike other parts of this book, you can answer the following questions in any order you wish. Some might be easier for you to answer first. Just please don't move on to the next step (Develop- ing Empathy [page 50]) until you've completed all of the questions from this step.

Reflection Questions

1. What were all of the positive qualities that drew you to your former partner in the beginning? Were they charming, motivated, funny, attractive, etc.?

2. What positive qualities did your partner have in the beginning that became negative later on or disappeared altogether? (For example, were you attracted to how career-focused they were early on but later that translated into them working long hours? Or were they very attentive in the beginning but later became controlling?)

3. What were the things you loved about your relationship with them? Did you like having a plus-one for events, a companion on weekends, a regular workout partner? Did you have similar goals or dreams? Did you like certain things you did with them or things you imagined you'd do in the future?

_____

_____

_____

_____

_____

_____

_____

_____

_____

_____

_____

_____

_____

_____

_____

_____

_____

_____

_____

_____

_____

_____

_____

4. What were the positive aspects of your relationship that later became negative or disappeared altogether? (For example, did you like having a workout partner but then you stopped enjoying that time together because they were overly critical of your weight? Or did you spend a lot of time together in the beginning only to rarely see each other later?)

_____

_____

_____

_____

_____

_____

_____

_____

_____

_____

_____

_____

_____

_____

_____

_____

_____

5. Write down all of the special moments you had with your former partner. Did they make a big deal about your birthday or always bring you coffee in the morning?

_____

_____

_____

_____

_____

_____

_____

_____

_____

_____

_____

_____

_____

_____

_____

_____

_____

_____

_____

_____

_____

_____

_____

6. Write down all the special moments that later became tainted for you. (For example, maybe they showed up for you in an important way, but then they threw it in your face later or expected something in return.)

7. What were all of the things (positive and negative) your friends and family said about your ex? Were there some things you heard that you ignored, rationalized, or excused?

_____

_____

_____

_____

_____

_____

_____

_____

_____

_____

_____

_____

_____

_____

_____

_____

_____

_____

_____

_____

_____

_____

_____

_____

_____

8. What were the things you disliked about your former partner?
Were they self-centered or self-seeking? Did they care a lot
about appearances? Were they very critical or negative?

_____

_____

_____

_____

_____

_____

_____

_____

_____

_____

_____

_____

_____

_____

_____

_____

_____

_____

_____

_____

_____

_____

9. What were the things you disliked about your relationship? Did you feel uncomfortable voicing your wants or needs? Did they get really mean or abusive when you fought? Did they refuse to take responsibility for an issue or apologize?

_____

_____

_____

_____

_____

_____

_____

_____

_____

_____

_____

_____

_____

_____

_____

_____

Congratulations! You've just finished a monumental step. Take some time to give yourself a pat on the back and be kind to yourself. Realistically narrating your toxic relationship is often a painful but necessary step in the healing process. Having a nuanced perspective of your toxic relationship will be helpful for you as you move forward.

Reflection Questions

When you're ready, look back over your answers to the previous questions and consider the following:

1. What do you think and feel about your ex today?

_____

_____

_____

_____

_____

_____

_____

_____

_____

_____

_____

_____

_____

_____

_____

_____

_____

2. Do you feel that the positives in the relationship outweighed the negatives? Why or why not?

3. What are things that you're still angry and hurt about today?

4. If you were to write a letter to your ex (and never send it to them), what would you say?

step 3: developing empathy

When I finally left my last toxic relationship, I was incredibly angry. I had a lot of anger against my former partner, but most of my anger was actually directed at myself.

I was angry that I had put up with so much for so long. I was angry that I had said yes when I should have said no. I was angry that I had stayed *years* past when I first felt like the relationship wasn't good for me. I was angry that I hadn't set boundaries, or that I'd set them and then never enforced them. I was also angry at myself for remaining silent to my friends and family about the true nature of that relationship.

While anger can be a great motivating force in making change in our lives, it can also lead to shame and other feelings of humiliation: *I should have known better. I'm such an idiot that I didn't leave sooner.*

As shown in multiple studies, shame doesn't help or motivate us to be better. Annette Kämmerer, who writes about the impacts of shame, said, "Shame makes us direct our focus inward and view our entire self in a negative light." In one study, it was found that those who experience shame are also much more likely to experience depression and other disorders and to adopt negative behaviors instead of positive ones.

We can move away from shame and toward a healthier sense of self by developing empathy, both for the self that was in the toxic relationship and the self we are trying to be today.

What Is Empathy?

Empathy consists of being sensitive to and vicariously experiencing the feelings of others. Many of us who have been in toxic relationships find that we have stopped having empathy for ourselves. We're no longer aware of or sensitive to our own feelings because we've spent so long being too tuned in to the feelings of others.

Developing empathy for yourself involves getting a full understanding of yourself as you were when you started your toxic relationship, when you left it, and then today. Having a good sense of empathy for yourself allows you to move away from shame and toward self-compassion.

Who You Were

Our relationships are never formed in a vacuum. They are often the result of a myriad of experiences, from childhood to today. When I first started dating my former partner, I had very few, if any, healthy relationship skills. I also had no healthy relationship role models. Because of this, I formed some beliefs about relationships, including that a relationship taking "work" meant things were supposed to be hard, and that all of my relationship issues could be fixed by reaching certain destinations (getting married, buying a home, having children, etc.). Looking back, it's not surprising that my relationships weren't all that healthy.

Reflection Questions

1. Thinking about relationships you saw growing up (either those of your parents, grandparents, aunts and uncles, close family friends, or from movies or books), what expectations, beliefs, or ideals did you have or learn from these relationships?

_____

_____

_____

_____

_____

_____

_____

_____

_____

_____

_____

_____

_____

_____

_____

_____

_____

_____

_____

_____

_____

_____

2. How would you have described a "normal" or "healthy" romantic relationship? Would you describe those the same or differently? Would you have those same beliefs about relationships today? Why or why not?

_____

_____

_____

_____

_____

_____

_____

_____

_____

_____

_____

_____

_____

_____

_____

_____

_____

_____

_____

_____

3. Do you feel that your beliefs or expectations around relation-ships "set you up" to choose your toxic partner? Or do you feel that you ended up in a toxic relationship despite having healthy relationship role models? If you could guess why you ended up in a toxic relationship, why would that be? Do you think you would make the same choices today? Why or why not?

4. What experiences (your relationship with your parents, prior partners, or other impactful people) uniquely shaped you to have the relationship you did with your toxic partner? (For example, one of your parents was an alcoholic, and then your former partner was one too.)

5. What did you think or imagine about your relationship when you first started dating your toxic partner? What did you hope or expect? Were these hopes or expectations grounded in reality? Why or why not?

_____

_____

_____

_____

_____

_____

_____

_____

_____

_____

_____

_____

_____

_____

_____

_____

_____

_____

_____

_____

_____

_____

_____

6. What helped you finally decide to leave your toxic partner? Was there a specific moment or several things all at once?

7. What were red flags or warning signs you missed or ignored when you started dating your toxic partner? What did you tell yourself about these when you discovered them later? (For example, *It will change after we have kids* or *It's not that bad*.)

8. What problems in your toxic relationship do you think resulted from your own issues or behaviors? (For example, maybe you struggled with resentment, voicing your needs, or enforcing boundaries.)

Becoming Who You Want to Be

While you may not be where you would like to be as far as relationship recovery or life situation go, you should have a better idea of who you could be and what you would likely need to do to get there.

Reflection Questions

1. Are you the same person today that you were when you started dating your toxic partner? Why or why not?

_____

_____

_____

_____

_____

_____

_____

_____

_____

_____

_____

_____

_____

_____

_____

_____

_____

2. What are some expectations, beliefs, or ideals you have about "normal" or "healthy" romantic relationships that you would like to give up?

_____

_____

_____

_____

_____

_____

_____

_____

_____

_____

_____

_____

_____

_____

_____

_____

_____

_____

_____

_____

_____

_____

3. What would you like your new expectations, beliefs, or ideals to be?

_____

_____

_____

_____

_____

_____

_____

_____

_____

_____

_____

_____

_____

_____

_____

_____

_____

_____

_____

_____

_____

4. What are some specific things that would help you become who you want to be? (For example, learning how to set and enforce boundaries, developing a self-care practice, etc.)

_____

_____

_____

_____

_____

_____

_____

_____

_____

_____

_____

_____

_____

_____

_____

_____

_____

_____

_____

_____

Evaluating Your Self-Talk

As you work on becoming who you want to be and developing more empathy for yourself, you need to evaluate how you talk to yourself on a regular basis. Our inner monologue is influenced by our beliefs. If you want to know what you believe about yourself, keep track of all of the thoughts that flit through your mind during the day. (For example, *I can't do that. I'm not enough. No one will ever love me.*) Your thoughts influence your actions. If you believe you're "too sensitive," for example, then you may do things to confirm that belief, such as not setting a boundary after a friend says something mean to you.

Below are some words you should be aware of when you say them to yourself or when you describe yourself to other people. Synonyms count too!

- Should
- Always
- Never
- Sensitive
- Stupid
- Alone
- Hopeless
- Lazy
- Dramatic
- Overreact
- Can't

Reflection Questions

1. What are statements you often say to yourself that use the words listed on the previous page?

_____

_____

_____

_____

_____

_____

_____

_____

_____

_____

_____

_____

_____

_____

_____

_____

_____

_____

_____

2. In what ways do you talk negatively to yourself? Would you ever talk to a friend the way you talk to yourself? Why or why not?

3. How could you rewrite those negative statements to be kinder or more positive? (For example, instead of, "I shouldn't have allowed them to control our finances," you could say, "I made a mistake, but I will make a healthier choice in the future.")

4. Write down five positive statements you would like to start saying to yourself instead. (For example, "I am enough.")

step 4:
softening
emotions

When we've been hurt, it's our tendency to put our guard up and numb out or shut down. We build a wall around ourselves that keeps others at a distance. We hope this wall will protect us from future emotional pain. We may say things like "I don't care," "I'm fine," or "It doesn't bother me." And we probably feel those things are true too.

While it's entirely natural to want to ward off future harm, hiding behind a wall actually hurts us in the long run. While we're avoiding negative feelings, we're also cutting off our ability to feel other emotions, even the good ones like excitement and joy. Plus, if we're walled off, we're preventing ourselves from having intimate and authentic relationships with others (not just romantic partners).

The way to avoid staying hardened and emotionless forever is to "soften" our emotions. To do this means we have to create a safe place for ourselves to be able to let down our defenses and feel our emotions however we need to.

No safety can exist in a toxic relationship. Feeling "safe" means that we are comfortable sharing our entire selves (fears, insecurities, hopes, dreams, etc.). Often in toxic relationships, our feelings were minimized or invalidated. We were told we "shouldn't be upset." Our boundaries were violated. We were rejected, criticized, blamed, shamed, and ignored.

Being in a toxic relationship for an extended period of time can also have a lasting impact on our relationship with ourselves. We may then, in turn, minimize and invalidate our own feelings. We may tell ourselves we "shouldn't keep thinking about it." We may also reject, criticize, blame, shame, and ignore ourselves and our needs, thoughts, and feelings.

Creating a Safe Space

We create emotional safety for ourselves when we care for ourselves and believe that we are deserving of that love and attention. We create emotional safety with another person when they care for us and we believe that we are deserving of their love and attention.

Reflection Questions

1. Do you care for yourself? Why or why not? How do you show that you care for yourself? Or what would you like to do to show that you care for yourself?

_____

_____

_____

_____

_____

_____

_____

_____

_____

_____

_____

_____

2. What negative beliefs do you have about or in response to reading that "we are deserving of that love and attention"? Do you believe you deserve your own love and attention? Why or why not?

_____

_____

_____

_____

_____

_____

_____

_____

_____

_____

_____

_____

_____

_____

_____

_____

_____

_____

3. Imagine you were to tell your best friend the kind of things you tell yourself. Could you say those things to them and about them? Why or why not?

4. In what negative ways do you judge yourself or your process, life, feelings, and choices?

5. How could you rewrite those to be more positive or more gentle? (For example, "I may not be where I'd like to be in my recovery process, but I'm taking positive steps toward it today.")

_____

_____

_____

_____

_____

_____

_____

_____

_____

_____

_____

_____

_____

_____

_____

_____

_____

_____

_____

_____

6. Take an inventory of your current relationships. Which ones make you feel emotionally safest?

7. List the things that make you feel emotionally unsafe. These are your "triggers." These could be judgmental comments or boundary violations. Be specific.

8. When you are triggered, you may need to work on managing your emotions, setting a boundary, or both. Pick a few of your triggers that happen the most often and brainstorm an action plan you could put into place when they happen. (For example, "I really don't want to see pictures of my ex with their current partner. I will unfollow, mute, or block them on social media.")

Letting Down Our Defenses

We create defenses because we're scared. We don't want to be hurt again, and if we are recovering from a toxic relationship, we have been hurt in the most vulnerable and tender parts of ourselves. We opened ourselves up to be known by another person, and that person hurt us.

Creating defenses looks like:

- not sharing honestly with ourselves or others ("I'm fine")
- isolating
- throwing ourselves into staying busy
- avoiding any kind of conflict
- taking our anger out on others (called "displacing")
- denying how we feel
- trying to intellectualize or justify what happened to us
- telling ourselves we "shouldn't" do something or feel a certain way (cry, be upset, etc.)
- acting like a victim (*Poor me. This always happens to me . . .*)
- numbing out or acting out in unhealthy ways (drinking, overeating, etc.)
- being passive-aggressive

Reflection Questions

1. What defenses have you put up? How have they helped you? How have they hurt you or others?

2. What would it feel like to no longer have your defenses up? What do you fear might happen?

3. Are your fears rational? Why or why not?

_____

_____

_____

_____

_____

_____

_____

_____

_____

_____

_____

_____

_____

_____

_____

_____

_____

_____

_____

_____

_____

_____

_____

_____

_____

4. What feelings have you tried to avoid, bury, numb, or ignore?

5. What things (music, movies, etc.) make you feel safe and warm? Can you start cultivating having them in your life more at this time? How?

It can be helpful to start letting down our defenses with ourselves first. This journal is one such place where you should feel safe to share honestly and completely. Don't judge or be harsh with yourself in this process. We all recover at different rates. What matters most is that we're putting in the work to get better. When you tell yourself things like, *Why is this still bothering me? Shouldn't I be over this by now? THEY did this to me. Why do I have to be the one to do this work?*, gently remind yourself that you deserve a healthy relationship with yourself and others. That only starts by healing the effects of the unhealthy one you were in before.

If you have safe people you can share yourself with, try letting your defenses down with them too. It can be hard to reach out, especially when we've been isolating, but if these people truly care about us, they will understand as long as we're honest. It can be helpful to say things like, "I'm sorry I've been so absent. I've been really struggling, and it's made me want to isolate. I hope you'll forgive me. How are you?" If we've hurt them, it would be good to make an honest apology. A good apology might sound like: "I'm sorry that I didn't call you when I knew you needed me. How can I make it right?" You own the behavior, don't make excuses, and ask how you can make amends.

We heal by having safe, healthy relationships. These can be ones with family, friends, or a trusted therapist, coach, or spiritual advisor.

Be aware that when you get triggered, you may want to hide behind your walls again. That's okay. But know that you can't and shouldn't hide behind your walls forever. Take that time to work on feeling safe, and then forge out again.

Feeling Our Emotions

Feeling our emotions is an important part of the healing process. Despite all of our efforts to avoid, numb, deny, or ignore our feelings, we'll have to acknowledge them eventually.

When I was recovering from my own toxic relationship, I felt like loneliness would swallow me heart first, so I spent as much time as possible running from any and all negative feelings. It felt like I was trying to run a marathon through mud, like I was fighting against something.

And I was. I was fighting against feeling.

Feeling terrified me. I thought once I let myself cry, I'd cry until I took my last breath. I thought if I let myself be angry, I'd burn down the world.

What I learned from giving myself the opportunity to feel is that I'm a lot stronger than I thought. I didn't die. I didn't burn down the world. What I thought would be so overwhelming wasn't that way at all. My fear of feeling was more intense than my actual feelings. It's like hearing a noise in the bushes and thinking it's a bear when it's really just a chipmunk.

"Containment" is a helpful way of dealing with negative emotions: you set aside time (it can be just one to two hours) to feel with no distractions or obligations. It can be helpful to schedule this time in advance; then, when a feeling comes up, write it down and tell yourself, "I'm going to feel this during my contained time."

Reflection Questions

1. What has been successful for you in the past to feel your feelings? (For example, have you vented to a safe friend or taken time to exercise?)

2. When you think about feeling anger, what would you like to do? Scream? Hit something? What's a way you could feel that while not hurting yourself or others?

3. When you think about feeling sadness, what would you like to do? Not move? Dissolve into a puddle? What's a way you could feel that without hurting yourself or others?

_____

_____

_____

_____

_____

_____

_____

_____

_____

_____

_____

_____

_____

_____

_____

_____

_____

_____

4. Plan your next "contained" feeling time. Schedule the time and day when you'll do it and commit to doing it the same time every week for however long you think you might need.

_____

_____

_____

_____

_____

_____

_____

_____

_____

_____

_____

_____

_____

_____

_____

_____

_____

_____

_____

_____

_____

_____

_____

_____

5. What will you do during that first time? What would you like to work through? Some ideas for "feeling" time: journaling, exercising, listening to music, breathing deeply, or allowing yourself to cry.

step 5:
accepting personal responsibility

"You're not owning your part in that relationship," a friend told me.

"What are you talking about?" I retorted. "I'm not the one who . . ." and then I listed off several of my former partner's offenses.

"I know he did. But that doesn't change the fact that he isn't even in the picture anymore and you're still miserable."

I looked at her silently for a moment. She was right, but I didn't want to acknowledge it then.

My first reaction when someone says something to me that might have some truth in it is to get defensive. Who wants to acknowledge when we are responsible? Isn't it easier to just blame someone else and ignore our own faults? Absolutely! But when we blame other people for our issues, our lives and relationships don't improve. In working with clients, I've seen this again and again.

We believe things like:

- "I don't need to change."
- "It's not my fault I'm like this."
- "It doesn't matter what I do. It's always going to end up the same way."
- "I/my relationships will always be like this."
- "I'll never be happy because nothing I do matters."

These kinds of beliefs set us up to be:

- chronically unhappy, anxious, and angry
- paralyzed by indecision and fear
- dependent on others for validation, assurance, and approval
- so fearful about making a mistake that we don't take any risks
- emotionally unhealthy

Accepting personal responsibility is the ultimate step in growing and changing. So what does accepting personal responsibility look like? It includes:

- owning and taking back your power
- acknowledging that you are solely responsible for your thoughts, feelings, actions, reactions, and choices
- no longer blaming others for your thoughts, feelings, actions, reactions, and choices
- accepting that your life can be what *you* make of it, regardless of your past and the choices of other people
- not taking the thoughts, feelings, actions, reactions, and choices of others personally
- honoring your limitations and weaknesses and celebrating your assets and strengths
- selecting positive affirmations that correct how you talk to yourself

Victim Mentality

Taking ownership of your own growth isn't easy, especially when you've been hurt, abused, or traumatized in a previous relationship. There are times when we have been victims. We were powerless and helpless. But there is a difference between being a victim and having a victim mentality.

We can honor that we were a victim (something was done *to* us that had devastating effects) while not having a victim mentality. We maintain a victim mentality when we believe that nothing we do will help and that the world is out to get us.

People are in a victim mentality when they:

- are unwilling to do any work to improve themselves and change
- regularly make up excuses or blame others ("I couldn't get here on time because the traffic was so bad" when you also didn't leave your home on time)
- refuse to develop appropriate coping skills
- would rather complain than look for possible solutions to problems
- feel helpless and powerless to make changes
- don't trust themselves and their choices

Reflection Questions

1. In what ways have you acted out of a victim mentality?

2. Are there things you have told yourself that make it difficult for you to accept personal responsibility? (For example, *I always have unhealthy relationships. Why try something different?*)

3. In what ways have you blamed others for things that you were actually responsible for?

_____

_____

_____

_____

_____

_____

_____

_____

_____

_____

_____

_____

_____

_____

_____

_____

_____

_____

_____

4. What have you complained about without seeking possible solutions?

_____

_____

_____

_____

_____

_____

_____

_____

_____

_____

_____

_____

_____

_____

_____

_____

_____

_____

_____

_____

_____

_____

_____

5. In what ways have you chosen to be unhappy? (For example, not applying for new jobs even though you aren't happy at your current one.)

_____

_____

_____

_____

_____

_____

_____

_____

_____

_____

_____

_____

_____

_____

_____

_____

_____

_____

_____

_____

_____

6. What things in your life have you said "yes" to that haven't been in your best interest? (For example, you agreed to volunteer at your children's school when you were already too strapped with other commitments.)

How to Start Accepting Personal Responsibility

Now let's look at how you can begin taking personal responsibility instead.

Reflection Questions

1. What are positive affirmations or beliefs you could start saying or writing that would counter what you have told yourself to avoid taking responsibility?

_____

_____

_____

_____

_____

_____

_____

_____

_____

_____

_____

_____

_____

_____

_____

_____

2. What kind of life would you like to have? How would it look? Where would you live? What would you be doing?

3. What are things you do that make you happy or things you used to do that made you happy? Can you schedule time soon to do them?

_____

_____

_____

_____

_____

_____

_____

_____

_____

_____

_____

_____

_____

_____

_____

_____

_____

_____

_____

step 5: accepting personal responsibility

1. What are things you could start saying "no" to that would help you spend more time doing what you love?

_____

_____

_____

_____

_____

_____

_____

_____

_____

_____

_____

_____

_____

_____

_____

_____

_____

_____

_____

_____

_____

_____

_____

_____

_____

One of the most powerful aspects of taking personal responsibility is in refusing to take personally how other people choose to respond, act, or react. If you were in a toxic relationship that included gaslighting (psychological manipulation that causes you to question the validity of your own thoughts and perceptions), this can be incredibly difficult to overcome. You may have been told things like, "You made me do that" or "Why do you always ruin things?" However, none of us can make anyone else respond, act, or react in a certain way. We aren't all-powerful.

What Is Not Your Responsibility

When anyone makes a choice or acts or reacts in a certain way, it's not so much about us as it is about them. What someone says and does is wholly their responsibility. For example, if you accidentally bumped into a stranger who then berated you for being a "terrible" person, you'd probably be able to brush it off. That person clearly isn't having a good day. *This isn't about me*, you'd think. *I barely bumped her, and she freaked out on me!* But if one of our loved ones reacts in a way that isn't proportionate to the event (such as freaking out over a minor mistake), we take it personally. We feel responsible for their emotional reaction.

Part of taking personal responsibility is in no longer accepting ownership for the actions of others. You didn't "make" that stranger freak out on you and neither are you responsible for all of the emotional reactions of your loved ones. You can't control how other people respond. You can only control how you respond.

Everything you do and say has consequences, but it's important to evaluate whether the consequences match or warrant what you did. If you said something hurtful, you should own it and apologize, but you don't deserve to be abused, attacked, or insulted.

Reflection Questions

1. In what ways have you taken responsibility for situations or events that weren't yours to take?

_____

_____

_____

_____

_____

_____

_____

_____

_____

_____

_____

_____

_____

_____

_____

_____

_____

_____

_____

_____

2. What are some questions you could ask yourself in the moment to help you assess whether something is your responsibility? (For example: Does the reaction seem appropriate to the event? Is this truly about me or them?)

_____

_____

_____

_____

_____

_____

_____

_____

_____

_____

_____

_____

_____

_____

_____

_____

_____

_____

_____

_____

_____

3. What are some affirmations you could start telling yourself to no longer take responsibility for others? (For example, *I can't control how other people act. I can only control myself.*)

_____

_____

_____

_____

_____

_____

_____

_____

_____

_____

_____

_____

_____

_____

_____

There are many things in life we have no control over. We get laid off because our company is closing down, for example. But we can decide to make what we can of what's happened. Instead of lying around and racking up debt, we could polish our resume and apply to new jobs. When we take personal responsibility, we positively create a life we want instead of feeling like nothing we do will make a difference.

step 6:
establishing accountability

Establishing accountability is the next step in accepting personal responsibility, and it requires getting support to help you own your healing journey. This is how you ensure that you grow and change. This can be helpful for you now and in the future.

An Accountability Source

Many of us do best when someone else helps us be accountable. We might call them our "accountability source." A boss, trusted friend, therapist, or coach may help us stay accountable to deadlines or goals, for example. When we have someone else as our accountability source, we check in with them on a regular basis, and they help us make sure we stick to what we've agreed to. They also provide honest feedback and have a desire to help us change. Progress is about recognizing when we've made a mistake, and instead of giving up, recommitting to our goals. An accountability source helps us do that.

As you continue healing from your toxic relationship, you will need accountability in making sure you don't fall back into old patterns. You will slip up—that's just part of being human. But the important thing is that you don't make something a habit again.

Reflection Questions

1. Do you have someone in your life who could hold you accountable to continue your healing process? If not, could you look into finding someone (such as a therapist or coach)?

2. What qualities would you want this accountability person to have? (For example, nonjudgmental, caring, empathetic, honest.)

3. What small goals would you like them to help you with? (For example, continuing to work through this book or learning positive communication skills.)

Clarifying Goals

Holding ourselves accountable takes work. As you begin to heal from your toxic relationship, you may find yourself less motivated to continue this work. You may:

- no longer feel the same urgency you did when you first got out of the relationship because you feel okay most days now
- feel like you haven't progressed "enough" or as "much" as you expected you would by this time
- think you don't need to recover anymore because you've recovered "enough"
- not feel clear anymore on what you need to work on
- not want to continue "reliving" what happened

The problem is, if we don't continue our healing process, we stall our growth. While you may have dealt with what you needed to in order to move forward, you may not have a clear plan to make sure you don't find yourself in another toxic relationship. It wouldn't be fair for me to help you heal from your toxic relationship, but land you in another one that you'll need to heal from again in the future!

Therefore, it's vital to get clear on your immediate, mid-range, and long-term goals.

Reflection Questions

1. What are goals you'd like to achieve in the next three months? (For example, start seeing a therapist, getting back to a hobby that you enjoy.)

---

2. What steps could you take to help you achieve those goals? (For example, research therapists, look into hobby meet-up groups in your area.)

3. What are goals you'd like to achieve in the next six months to a year? (For example, develop closer friendships, start dating, have a regular plan for self-care.)

_____

_____

_____

_____

_____

_____

_____

_____

_____

_____

_____

_____

_____

_____

_____

_____

_____

_____

_____

_____

_____

_____

4. What steps could you take to help you achieve those goals? (For example, commit to texting your friends at least three times a week and seeing them once a week, sign up for a dating app, plan a daily walk with a neighbor.)

5. What are goals you'd like to achieve in the next five to ten years? (For example, purchase a home, have a long-term healthy relationship.)

6. What are steps you could take to help you achieve those goals? (For example, start saving, see a therapist with your current partner to learn new relationship skills.)

7. Why are these goals important to you? How will your life be positively impacted by following through on these goals?

Refer back to these goals often. It can be helpful to keep them somewhere you can look at them regularly, such as on your nightstand or in the notes app on your phone.

Staying Honest

Remaining accountable to yourself and others requires a high degree of honesty. You have to learn to be honest about how and what you're doing, even when you don't want to. When you fall into certain traps of avoidance, you have to recognize them and then get back on track.

Reflection Questions

1. What do you usually do to try to avoid doing something else? Do you make up excuses, ignore phone calls or texts, find yourself saying "yes" to too many things, get really busy?

2. What routines could you put in place to help you stay on task with your goals? Could you put reminders in your calendar, set up regular check-in times with your accountability source, or start a daily journaling practice?

3. When is it hard for you to be honest with others? Why do you think that is?

4. What might you need in order to feel more comfortable being honest? (For example, having the other person be gentle with you and not judgmental.)

5. Why is it important that you be honest with yourself and others?

step 7: restoring trust

While in my last toxic relationship and long after, I didn't trust myself to make even small choices. I was indecisive and often looked to other people to make decisions for me. I was at a loss to figure out even what I wanted to eat on a given day.

Learning to Trust Yourself

It's not surprising that I struggled with trusting myself. My track record showed that I'd made many poor decisions, including picking and staying with several toxic and even abusive partners. I'd also been gaslighted so often that I doubted my own perception of reality.

Here are signs that you too may struggle with trusting yourself:

- You struggle with making any kind of decision, big or small.
- You tend to be so paralyzed by making a "wrong" decision that you make none at all (which is, in itself, a decision).
- You are controlling of other people, places, things, and your environment because it makes you feel safe.
- You minimize or ignore your own needs and desires.
- You struggle to speak up for yourself.
- You wait for "the other shoe to drop" by constantly expecting the worst.
- You constantly reflect on your negative experiences to reinforce why you shouldn't make decisions for yourself.
- You interrogate other people on what they think you should do.
- You participate in self-sabotaging behaviors.
- You say "yes" when you mean "no," and then may fail to keep the commitments you have made to yourself and others.

- You let other people make decisions for you.
- You listen to people's words over paying attention to their actions.
- You fail to listen to your gut or intuition.
- You frequently use language that reinforces your lack of choice: "I couldn't . . . ," "I can't . . . ," "I *had* to . . . ," "I was powerless," etc.

Reflection Questions

1. Do you trust yourself today? Why or why not? Which traits from the above list resonate with you?

_____

_____

_____

_____

_____

_____

_____

_____

_____

_____

_____

_____

_____

_____

2. When is the last time you made a decision for yourself (small or big)? What was the result? How did the result of that decision inform your future choices?

3. What scares you the most about trusting yourself?

Restoring trust in yourself starts with prioritizing your own needs and safety. Trusting yourself looks like:

- practicing self-care
- treating yourself with kindness and love
- consistently doing things that align with your own morals and values
- being aware of your thoughts and feelings
- expressing what you feel, need, and want to those around you, regardless of their reactions
- pursuing your own goals and dreams
- believing that you can survive and thrive even through tough times

Evaluate Your Thoughts

We've talked extensively about how you talk to yourself. This remains one of the most powerful ways to change the core beliefs that surround your lack of self-trust.

When you make a mistake or try to pursue a goal, you may find that the cruel inner critic residing in your brain starts running its mouth: "Of course you made a mistake. You're always making mistakes!" or "That goal is stupid. You'll never reach it anyway."

If you had a close friend that was speaking to themselves that way, what would you say? It's likely you'd compassionately offer something more positive, like, "Yes, you made a mistake, but you need to keep trying! It's all about progress," or "That goal is *not* stupid because it's something you've always dreamed of. Keep at it! Don't give up!"

You can learn to speak to yourself with the same compassion you'd offer to a close friend. You don't have to let your cruel inner critic remain unchecked. You deserve the same compassion that you would offer anyone else, and that is key to beginning to trust yourself again.

Start Small

If you've been discounting your thoughts, needs, dreams, and desires for a while now, the idea of making a big decision may feel overwhelming. It can be helpful to start making decisions in small ways and build up from there.

Even if it's just saying "yes" or "no" when someone asks you if you would like a receipt, it can help you begin to feel comfortable voicing what you would or wouldn't like. Anytime you make a decision that goes well, it reinforces that you can make decisions for yourself and that you should trust your inner guidance.

Reflection Questions

1. What is something small that you could start taking ownership of making decisions about?

2. How will you begin? How can you stay accountable and keep making decisions for yourself?

Figuring Out Your Boundaries

The biggest consequence of not trusting yourself is that you often say "yes" to things that drain you. This can happen in any situation or relationship: at work, with family, with friends, and with romantic partners.

Most people don't quite understand what a boundary is, so let's define it. In personal relationships, a boundary delineates what you can control and what you can't. An example of a personal boundary is, "I do not respond to texts or phone calls after 10 p.m. because that's when I need to go to bed."

Boundaries are not ultimatums. They aren't insurmountable walls that people have to climb over to be able to have a relationship with you. They don't control the behaviors of others, and they don't allow you to be used or abused.

Imagine that you have a Hula-Hoop around yourself. Everything that's inside of your Hula-Hoop is what you can control; it's your boundary. This includes your thoughts, actions, reactions, desires, dreams, goals, and decisions. Everyone else is responsible for everything within their own Hula-Hoop. This includes their thoughts, actions, reactions, desires, dreams, goals, and decisions.

What Are Healthy Boundaries?

There are three boundary styles.

- **Porous:** If you have porous boundaries, you have no to very few boundaries. You often overstep the boundaries of others, and you let other people overstep yours. You tend to "drop" your Hula-Hoop and try to get into others' or you let people get into yours.

- **Rigid:** If you have rigid boundaries, you tend to keep people at a distance or push them away entirely. You struggle asking for help and being vulnerable or intimate with others. Your Hula-Hoop isn't a small, thin piece of plastic but a brick wall that prevents you from connecting emotionally with others and them with you.

- **Healthy:** If you have healthy boundaries, you allow for flexibility, you communicate clearly about what is and isn't okay for you, and you value the needs and opinions of others. You're clearly positioned in your Hula-Hoop, and you let everyone else be in theirs.

Many of us with unhealthy boundaries vacillate between having a porous and a rigid boundary style. We have no boundaries, which means we are constantly drained and exhausted while trying to control and change other people, or we are extremely protective of ourselves in a way that keeps everyone out. We may jump between the two styles whenever we experience a consequence (like being too exhausted to continue to say yes or getting tired of not having intimate relationships).

Having healthy boundaries starts with being clear with yourself about your needs and recognizing that they matter. In answering the following questions, please consider all of your relationships (work, family, friends, and romantic partners).

Reflection Questions

1. What do you need in your relationships? What do you like and dislike? What are you comfortable with and what are you not?

_____

_____

_____

_____

_____

_____

_____

_____

_____

_____

_____

_____

_____

_____

_____

_____

_____

_____

_____

_____

_____

_____

_____

2. What scares you in relationships? What specific things trigger your fear?

3. Why do your needs matter in a relationship? How does prioritizing your needs help you get the kind of relationships you want?

How to Set Boundaries

Boundaries always need to be stated specifically, simply, and clearly. It can also help to communicate the consequence that will happen if the boundary is violated. Here are some boundary scripts:

"I need . . ." (I need you to get this done by 5 p.m. today.)

"I would like . . ." (I would like to leave your sister's house by 7 p.m. I have to get to bed early tonight.)

"Could you . . ." (Could you wake up the kids tomorrow morning?)

"I will . . ." (I will start doing all of the laundry, but that means I will no longer have time to do the dishes too.)

"I won't . . ." (I won't tolerate yelling. If it happens, I will no longer participate in the conversation.)

"I can . . ." (I can listen to you complain for one minute, but if you're not willing to brainstorm solutions, I won't be able to continue to listen.)

"I can't . . ." (I can't help you lie to your boss.)

"I'm . . ." (I'm only able to work for five hours next week.)

Healthy boundaries are flexible, but to a point. Some boundaries you may be able to compromise on. For example, you may want to leave your partner's sister's house at 7 p.m., but your partner would like to stay until 8. You could compromise and leave at 7:30 instead. Other boundaries you won't and shouldn't compromise on (like any kind of behavior that makes you feel unsafe, abused, or used).

Reflection Questions

1. What boundaries do you need to set? Who do you need to set them with?

2. How will you set them? What will you say? When do you plan on doing this?

3 How will you have accountability to make sure you follow
through with setting your boundaries?

How to Enforce Boundaries

Another important aspect of boundaries is that we should never set a boundary we aren't able or willing to enforce. If we set a boundary that we don't follow through on enforcing, we teach ourselves and others that our words and our needs don't matter.

Enforcing boundaries usually involves temporarily withdrawing from a situation or person. This can be incredibly uncomfortable. We also may not want to deal with the uncomfortable feelings that arise when someone else experiences a consequence like us withdrawing. ("Why can't you be here for me? I need you!" someone might say, even though they were just yelling at you, and you told them you won't tolerate yelling.)

Reflection Questions

1. What do you think will be difficult for you in enforcing boundaries? What scares you about enforcing them?

2. What would help or support you in enforcing certain boundaries? (For example, perhaps you can reach out to an accountability source or work on a hobby that is soothing after you have enforced a tough boundary.)

3. What statements could you tell yourself when you are scared or uncomfortable about enforcing a boundary? (For example, *Healthy relationships have boundaries. I need my boundaries to be honored in order to feel safe in my relationships.*)

_____

_____

_____

_____

_____

_____

_____

_____

_____

_____

_____

_____

_____

_____

_____

_____

_____

_____

_____

_____

_____

Develop a Self-Care Plan

Often in toxic relationships, we give up our most valuable relationship: the one with ourselves. The way we get back to that is in prioritizing our own self-care, in setting goals around specific areas and sticking to them.

Reflection Questions

1. What do you like to do when you need to take care of yourself or you're struggling with something? Would you consider that a healthy habit that you would like to continue? Why or why not?

_____

_____

_____

_____

_____

_____

_____

_____

_____

_____

_____

_____

_____

_____

2. What are things you'd like to start doing that regularly bring you joy and peace? (For example, hanging out with friends more regularly, taking walks outside.)

_____

_____

_____

_____

_____

_____

_____

_____

_____

_____

_____

_____

_____

_____

_____

_____

_____

_____

_____

3. Are there things that you're doing currently that prevent you from practicing self-care? (For example, volunteering at your church several days a week or not bringing your lunch to work.)

4. How could you start *stopping* those things in order to make room for what you'd actually like to start doing?

_____

_____

_____

_____

_____

_____

_____

_____

_____

_____

_____

_____

_____

_____

_____

_____

_____

_____

_____

_____

_____

_____

_____

Below is a sample self-care plan with recommendations. Write down your own goals for what you would like for your plan.

Self-Care Plan

Type	Recommendations	Goals (daily or weekly)
Sleep	Get 7 to 9 hours per night (from __ p.m. to __ a.m.) Have a consistent routine, even on weekends Avoid electronics before bed	
Nutrition	Eat real foods Avoid sugar, caffeine, and alcohol	
Exercise	Get 30 minutes of cardiovascular exercise three times per week	
Socializing	Connect with at least one person per day Schedule at least one outing per week Spend time with nature and animals	
Relaxation	Practice yoga Take Epsom salt baths Go for a walk	

Type	Recommendations	Goals (daily or weekly)
Emotional Regulation	Practice self-awareness Employ positive thinking strategies Practice being flexible Practice self-soothing techniques	
Self-Development	Work with a therapist or coach Work toward a life goal Practice daily affirmations	
Mental Well-Being	Continue education courses Read books on new and interesting subjects Start a new hobby Practice gratitude	
Spiritual Well-Being	Spend time in nature Journal or pray Meditate Do things connected to your sense of purpose	

Post this self-care plan somewhere you can see it regularly. Again, it helps to have the reminder and to assess when you've fallen off track.

Choose You

I never chose myself in my toxic relationships. I chose my partner or our relationship over myself, my dreams, my goals, and my needs. So, my last bit of advice is to choose you. This means:

- choosing to be transparent with yourself and others, even when it is uncomfortable
- sharing yourself in a way that builds intimate relationships while also having clear boundaries
- respecting yourself and others
- testing your assumptions and self-talk by asking yourself whether you have evidence to support those beliefs
- listening to and honoring your intuition

Reflection Questions

1. How have you *not* chosen yourself? How has that impacted you negatively?

2. How will you start choosing yourself? What will it look like when you choose you?

_____

_____

_____

_____

_____

_____

_____

_____

_____

_____

_____

_____

_____

_____

_____

_____

_____

_____

_____

_____

3. What will be uncomfortable for you in choosing yourself? How can you overcome that discomfort?

4. How will you stay in tune with yourself to make sure you're trusting yourself and making the right decisions for you?

_____

_____

_____

_____

_____

_____

_____

_____

_____

_____

_____

_____

_____

_____

_____

_____

_____

_____

_____

_____

Choosing yourself on a regular basis is a feat. It's a triumph. It takes considerable healing and trust to get there, and I'm certain you will.

keep
healing

Congratulations! By finishing this guided journal, you've made valuable and incredible steps in your own healing process. Take some time to reflect on this journey and decide what you can do to continue your healing.

Healing Is a Journey

Healing is a journey, not a destination. Many of us make huge changes while we're single only to learn there is *more* work to do once we get into another relationship. I found that my bar of what was "normal" was considerably skewed once I got into a healthy relationship. I actually *thanked* a romantic partner for not yelling at me!

Reflection Questions

1. What did you realize about your past self while you worked through this journal? Did you make any discoveries that were surprising?

2. Is there anything that you've started doing differently? What did you think about those new actions? How have they made you feel?

3. What are some things you now know you need to learn more about or keep working on? (For example, setting and enforcing boundaries, having a self-care practice, etc.) What will you do to keep moving forward in those areas?

_____

_____

_____

_____

_____

_____

_____

_____

_____

_____

_____

_____

_____

_____

_____

_____

_____

_____

4. How have you been feeling since you started working through this journal? How are you today? Do you feel more positive or hopeful overall?

5. How do you now view your relationship with your former partner? Do you have the same feelings about them and your relationship as you did when you started this journal? Why or why not?

6. What chapters did you find the most difficult to work through? Why do you think that was?

7. What are you most looking forward to now?

If you find yourself struggling again, read your answers to some of the prompts in previous chapters and see how you'd respond to them today. Do you feel the same? Different? Is there something you've stopped doing that would be good for you to start up again? You can also return to your self-care plan and your goals for your future. Have you stopped doing anything that you need to restart?

Know that a sign of progress is when you make *new* mistakes. Yes, you'll still make mistakes because you're human, but making *new* mistakes means you're taking risks and trying something new instead of repeating the same behaviors over and over again.

Healing is like going up or down a spiral staircase. As you keep learning and implementing new strategies, you keep taking steps upward. If you stop working or even regress, you take steps down. All the while, you'll find that you keep encountering the same kind of issues or situations. How you handle those issues or situations will depend on where you are in your healing journey.

Also consider journaling as a daily practice for getting in touch with your thoughts and feelings. It can be helpful to journal at the same time every day (like the morning) and having a page or time goal, such as, "I will journal until I've completed two pages or 30 minutes."

Be kind to yourself. You've made considerable strides by completing this journal. Celebrate where you are today and don't stop striving to be healthier and happier.

I'm honored you chose to work through this journal. Know that I'm cheering you on, wherever you are. I am so proud of you.

resources

Codependent No More by Melody Beattie: If you struggle with setting and enforcing boundaries, this book can help you get there.

Facing Codependence by Pia Mellody: Like Beattie's book, Mellody expands on the topic of codependency and boundary-setting.

Nonviolent Communication: A Language of Life by Marshall Rosenberg: This book can help you learn how to be clear and assertive in your communication in a way that is beneficial for understanding.

Couple Skills: Making Your Relationship Work by Matthew McKay, et al.: Whether you're currently in a relationship or not, this book teaches how to communicate, solve problems, manage conflict, and connect with a romantic partner in easily actionable ways.

references

"Black and White Thinking." WebMD, October 25, 2021, www.webmd.com/mental-health/black-and-white-thinking.

Glass, Lillian. *Toxic People: 10 Ways of Dealing with People Who Make Your Life Miserable*. New York: St. Martin's Press, 1997.

Gregory, Andrew. "The Best Way to Get Over a Breakup, According to Science." *Time*, May 29, 2018, time.com/5287211/how-to-get-over-a-breakup.

The Gottman Institute (Gloria Willcox), "The Feeling Wheel," https://cdn.gottman.com/wp-content/uploads/2020/12/The-Gottman-Institute_The-Feeling-Wheel_v2.pdf.

Hart, S., and T. Hart. "The Future of Cognitive Behavioral Interventions within Behavioral Medicine." *Journal of Cognitive Psychotherapy: An International Quarterly* 24, no. 4 (2010): 344–353.

Kämmerer, Annette. "The Scientific Underpinnings and Impacts of Shame." *Scientific American*, August 9, 2019, www.scientificamerican.com/article/the-scientific-underpinnings-and-impacts-of-shame.

Langeslag, S. J. E., and M. E. Sanchez. "Down-Regulation of Love Feelings After a Romantic Break-Up: Self-Report and Electrophysiological Data." *Journal of Experimental Psychology: General* 147, no. 5 (2018): 720–733.

Layous, K., et al. "Delivering Happiness: Translating Positive Psychology Intervention Research for Treating Major and Minor Depressive Disorders." *Journal of Alternative and Complementary Medicine* 17, no. 8 (2011): 675–683.

Lightsey, O. R., et al. "Can Positive Thinking Reduce Negative Affect?: A Test of Potential Mediating Mechanisms." *Journal of Cognitive Psychotherapy: An International Quarterly* 26, no. 1 (2012): 71–88.

McKay, M., et al. *Thoughts and Feelings: Taking Control of Your Moods and Your Life*, 4th ed. Oakland, CA: New Harbinger, 2011.

Mellody, Pia, et al. *Facing Codependence*. New York: HarperCollins, 2011.

Newman, C. F., and A. T. Beck. "Cognitive Therapy." In *Kaplan and Sadock's Comprehensive Textbook of Psychiatry*, 9th ed., vol 2., edited by B. J. Sadock et al., 2857–2873. Philadelphia: Lippincott Williams & Wilkins, 2009.

"Shame and Guilt: The Good, the Bad, and the Ugly." *ResearchChannel*, February 9, 2008, www.youtube.com/watch?v=febgutDYP7w&feature=youtu.be.

acknowledgments

Many thanks to Madeline Greenhalgh and the rest of the staff at Page Street for giving me the opportunity to write a book on a topic that's sorely needed for many of us. It's a gift to be able to come out on the other side of a toxic relationship, and I hope this book helps many of you get there.

I'm also indebted to all of the clients I've been honored to work with. Without your trust in me, this book would never have happened.

Thank you to my wonderful husband, Brian, who is my biggest cheerleader and fan, and to our four children (Blaise, Jack, Lily, and Brienne), who make our life a beautiful kind of chaotic.

Many thanks as well to my dear friends whose support I can always count on: Kristen Bergstein, Kerry Kerr McAvoy, Kelly Eden, and anyone else I may have missed.

about the author

Tara Blair Ball is a certified relationship coach and author of *Grateful in Love: A Daily Gratitude Journal for Couples*. Ball specializes in helping individuals and couples go from toxic to happy. She has a bachelor's degree from Rhodes College (2008) and a master's from the University of Memphis (2012), along with coaching certifications from Transformation Academy and courses fully accredited by the Complementary Therapists Accredited Association (CTAA). She lives outside Memphis, Tennessee, with her husband, Brian, and their four children. When Ball isn't coaching clients, writing, or filming content, you can find her reading a sci-fi novel. If you want to discover other tools for healing and improving the relationships in your life, find her on Instagram and TikTok at @tara.relationshipcoach or her website at www.tararelationshipcoach.com.